Ornament at Harvard

John T. O'Connor

Editor

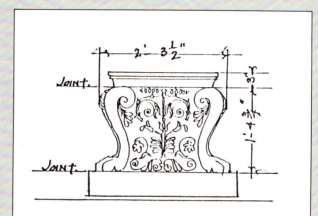

THREE QUARTER INCH SCALE DETAIL OF SEAT AT ENTRANCE TO HARVARD ARCHITECTURAL SCHOOL · CAMBRIDGE · MASS ··

Margaret Reeve
Publisher

Ornament and Crime

Adolf Loos

1908

In the modernist framework, ornament was form that did not follow function. Yet, except during this style's brief period of dominance, ornament traditionally fulfilled a particular function, orthogonal to the purpose of whatever object it adorned; it showcased the artist or architect's virtuosity, and created a deeper meaning for the functional object hosting it. Visual and linguistic symbols encoded in ornament can link a decorated object to a cultural or spatial context. A clear example of this can be found in Owen Jones' *The Grammar of Ornament*, a mid-19th century compendium of ornament and exotic polychromy. This work, which connects embellishments with their places of origin, influenced the highly idiosyncratic designs of Louis Sullivan, and he in turn the work of the Prairie School architects. A thistle motif found repeated within a building of the early 20th-century, therefore, could represent that structure's relationship with the surrounding prairie. In a similar fashion, a visual link can be made between the medievalist manifesto John Ruskin projected in his *The Seven Lamps of Architecture,* and the realization of these ideals at Harvard within the Venetian Gothic walls of Ware and Van Brunt's Memorial Hall. Ornament does not always follow this pattern, however. Frequently only the artist knows the significance of pictorial components of an embellishment. Why, for example did McKim, Mead and White choose three lions for fountainheads on the Bradley Memorial (pg.30)? In cases such as this, we may only label the artist's work whimsy.

As seen in many of the objects represented in this book, ornament can be anonymous, or it can be the hallmark of a highly individual expression. One need only look to H. H. Richardson's Austin Hall for an example of unmistakable personal style. On the whole, the most interesting and characteristic aspects of ornament at Harvard are its diversity and its idiosyncratic nature.

It is these aspects that makes a collection of embellishments at Harvard particularly important. By supporting a faculty whose work covers the breadth of their respective fields, Harvard has fostered and encouraged diversity, and is often found embracing divergent theories simultaneously. What other university could house the architectural circus that is Quincy Street lined with the work of McKim, Mead and White, Le Corbusier, H. H. Richardson and James Stirling among others? What other institution could present this street as a venerable jewel box of design theories—which indeed it is? Creativity and energy have always been in abundance within the University, and with these virtues present, permanent as well as ephemeral works continue to hold something not only for the mind, but for the soul as well.

John T. O'Connor

METAL

Gargoyle, sheet copper, Memorial Hall, 1868, now in collection of H.U.A.M.

For architectural purposes, metalwork, like carved stone, reached its apogee at Harvard between 1850 and 1925. Elaborate wrought iron and copper cresting once adorned the Flemish outlines of Weld Hall, as well as Matthews, Memorial Hall and the Newell boat house. Beyond constructional uses, metalwork was integrated on a personal level through smaller, more intimate objects. As the following pages illustrate, silver, bronze and gold have all been exploited by various artists and artisans in the creation of decorative sculpture and memorials. From anthropomorphic bronze monsters to a precious bejeweled cup, metal has been beaten, gilded, twisted, and burnished. . . .

The opal that Douglas Donaldson used for the finial atop this cup provided the inspiration for the bird motifs in the colored enamel plaques that adorn the bowl and stem. Donaldson made the cup as an exhibition piece for the Panama-California Exposition at San Diego, where it won a gold medal in 1915. After the Exposition closed, Donaldson organized a traveling exhibition of California crafts that was displayed in several eastern cities. While the show was at the Society of Arts and Crafts, Boston, this cup was bought to be used as a trophy for the winner of the singing competition held annually among the three new freshman dormitories on the river: Gore, Standish and Smith.

Edward S. Dodge, Class of 1873, president of the Alumni Chorus, had envisioned as the award a silver miniature of the Choragic Monument of Lysicrates, but this covered cup was selected instead, and the shield and motto added. Professor Elliot Forbes speculates: "The cup was presumably retired when singing ceased to be considered a competitive sport among freshmen."

Louise Todd Ambler

Cup with cover   Douglas Donaldson, 8 3/8″, silver, parcel-gilt, with enamels and semi-precious stones

Adolphus Busch Hall, designed to house the collections of Harvard's Germanic Museum, is an earnest, stern building. For some seventy years it has tried to exemplify the noblest achievements of German culture. Its stately sequence of interior spaces is as serious as its grand exterior and uplifting ornament.

Alongside carved figures of *Niebelungen* heroes and others, the facade carries four solemn inscriptions. *Du kannst, denn Du sollst* ("You can, because you ought") echoes Kant. *Kunst ist Können* ("Art is ability") goes back to Goethe. *Die That ist alles, nichts der Ruhm* ("The deed is everything, fame nothing") comes from Goethe's *Faust*. And *Es ist der Geist, der sich de Körper baut* ("The spirit creates the body") is quoted from Schiller's *Wallenstein's Tod*.

In a sense, these cliched quotations are as much second-hand copies of originals as were the plaster casts that formed the focus of the Museum's collection under its founder, Kuno Francke, Professor of the History of German Culture at Harvard. It was he who chose the cautionary tags, and it was no doubt he who selected the bronze lion to preside over the shadeless courtyard. It suits the admonitory, assertive character of the building. "The heraldic rigidity and archaic fierceness of the animal," he wrote of this copy of the lion that the Duke of Saxony had placed in front of his Brunswick castle in 1166, "make it peculiarly well fitted to stand here as a kind of architectural house dog guarding treasures of the past."

Time has undermined the highmindedness of Adolphus Busch Hall (not to mention its functionality as a museum). The development of German history in our century makes it difficult to take the moral claims of the building at face value. For it to survive as more than a quaint, mildly irritating relic, it must find a new, self-critical, perhaps even ironic stance. For that, it may need new ornament: maybe some quotations from Heinrich Heine and Walter Benjamin? And a fragment of the Berlin Wall in the courtyard?

Peter Nisbet

Lion, bronze with limestone base, replica of original dating from 1166, gift of Duke John Albert of Mecklenburg and the Duchy of Brunswick

When you enter the courtyard of the Harvard Biological Laboratories complex, it is a pair of bronze Great Indian rhinoceri, poised like sentinels flanking the central doors, which instantly dominate the setting. Sculpted by Katherine Lane in 1931 "to represent the perfect unusual animal not often seen," the life-sized rhinos were named for British queens: "Bessie, who gave me no end of trouble and Victoria of calm disposition."

An excellent example of the "industrial Harvard building type" designed by Coolidge, Shepley, Bulfinch and Abbott, the Harvard Biological Laboratories opened in September 1931. On either side of the central building, a wing extends forward to define the courtyard enclosure. Adorning the upper rim of the three facades is a freize of animals representing four regions of the world: neotropical, holarctic, Indo Asiatic and Ethiopian. The lively procession was cut into the brick with unusually broad, slanting strokes, with each line highlighted and activated by shadow in the later Han period style.

When Lane's creative talent focussed on the bronze trio of entrance doors, she conceived a design "to represent the sea, land and air as seen under the microscope or magnifying glass. I was anxious to have all the designs for the three doors of equal strength so the eye would not center on any single point of interest but see the doors as one." A concern with balance, harmony and style is displayed in Lane's intuitively accurate schemes. Although she had no previous understanding of evolution, she miraculously chose correct representations of lower to higher plants, terrestrial anthropods (insects) and marine invertebrates. Mounted in glass against a brick background, each door is divided into eight equal squares with inset circles. Every circle contains an elegant biological rendition. Behind the steel frame of each door a glass panel allows safe passage to and from the building. This combination of steel and glass also serves an important aesthetic function in lightening the staunchly heavy central solids. Not only are the doors visually attractive, but in being partially transparent, they command attention, enliven the otherwise static facade, and invite inspection.

Victoria Crowninshield Drake

Doors, bronze with circular glass panels, Katherine Lane, c. 1931

ird of infinite wisdom,

the meditative Ibis

presides over Lampy's Castle,

gently reminding passersby

that all is Vanitas.

Ornamental letter-form by Charles Allerton Coolidge, Class of 1881

Henry N. Cobb

Ibis pinnacle, copper, Harvard Lampoon, Wheelwright and Haven, 1909

Gargoyle, sheet copper, Claverly Hall, George Fogerty, architect, 1892

Gargoyle, sheet copper, Memorial Hall, 1868, now in collection of H.U.A.M.

Construction of the Fly Club Gate began in 1914 with a grant provided by the club's membership. The gate was erected facing the Charles River between Gore and Standish Halls, both designed by Shepley, Rutan & Coolidge and completed in 1913, which were originally freshman dormitories. Built on a more human scale than some of the other river gates, the gentle inward curve of this English Baroque gate conveys a sense of friendly beckoning. Its size and form mimic the Winthrop Gate, executed the same year, which faces the Fly Club Gate 150 feet to the south. In the Fly Club Gate, the judicious use of brick and picturesque wrought—iron detailing render the entrance less forbidding than, for example, the massive stone entrance and wrought-iron gate at Dunster House. The completed gate was photographed and published for the first time in the *Harvard Class Album of 1915*. The symbol of the Fly Club, the panther, is centered within the polychromed ironwork above the entry. Inscribed below the symbol is the dedication: "FOR FRIENDSHIPS MADE IN COLLEGE THE FLY CLUB IN GRATITUDE HAS BUILT THIS GATE."

John T. O'Connor

Detail, Fly Club Gate, c. 1914

STONE

Detail of revised elevation drawing, Robinson Hall, 1909, McKim, Mead and White, architects

In terms of architectural detail, Harvard's most opulent years began in 1838 with the rather awkward, early Gothic Revival Gore Hall. The next hundred years, one of the most feverish periods of growth at the University, would witness the realization of a plethora of architectural styles. Harvard projects embodied many of the mid-nineteenth century's picturesque styles, from the bristling surface of Ware and Van Brunt's Ruskinian Gothic Memorial Hall (1866) to the changeful outline of Peabody and Stearn's Hemenway gymnasium (1878) — a building of Queen Anne design virtually swathed in decoration. Carved stone and varied surfaces were an integral part of the design solutions during this epoch, and continued to be employed until the dawn of the International Style at Harvard in 1938.

John Ruskin, elaborating on his ideas of a wall as a curtain or "Wall Veil," wrote in *The Stones of Venice* that "a wall has no business to be dead . . . it ought to have members in its make, and purpose in its existence, like an organized creature, and to answer its end in a living and energetic way; and it is only when we do not choose to put any strength or organization into it, that it offends us by its deadness."

The walls of H. H. Richardson's Austin Hall at Harvard, completed in 1884, are very much alive, and by their many-faceted nature demand attention and inspection. Constructed of richly contrasting stone that has been shaped, layered, battered, staggered and woven into horizontal lines and counterpoint areas of pattern, Austin Hall represents a culmination of Richardson's mature style. In his conception, he surely was aware of Gottfried Semper's writing on "Der Vier Elemente der Baukunst" (1851), in which the author outlines his theory of the basic elements of architecture. Each element is linked to a specific technical process— ceramics, carpentry, weaving and masonry—whereby the "memory" of the process is preserved in the actual work. Semper wrote, "The tapestry remains the Wall's Primordial Sheath, and even when the erection of a solid wall is necessary, this remains only an invisible scaffolding, concealed behind the true and legitimate representation of the wall, the colorfully-worked tapestry."

For Semper, Ruskin and also Parisian architect Henri Labrouste, who developed a highly complex system of ornaments that Richardson became aware of as a student at the Ecole des Beaux Arts, the experience of an ornamented wall was a mental as well as a visual process that transformed a building into a monumental and symbolic object.

The mass of Austin Hall's exterior walls is lightened by means of stone coursing that strongly emphasizes the horizontal, thereby lifting the building above the earth and directing the eye to the central arched entry. This banding continues on the east and west solid end walls as a checkerboard quilt of light and dark Longmeadow sandstone with an inscription: "and thou shalt teach them ordinances and law and shalt show them the way wherein they must walk and the work that they must do."

William Drake

Detail, Austin Hall, c. 1885 from *Monographs of American Architecture I*

The exquisite carving found on both the exterior and interior stonework at Austin Hall represents the work of architect Henry Hobson Richardson at his finest. Austin Hall, completed in 1881, presents itself at once as both a classically sedate yet striking image even to the untrained eye. The architect employed color in a mosaic—like manner and combined this with smooth, richly carved and rusticated surfaces, creating a lively surface skin that fairly bristles with activity, tempered only by the brilliant simplicity of the building's overall form. The polychromy of Austin Hall may borrow something from Van Brunt's Memorial Hall, finished only three years earlier, but does not share in the Gothic Revival frenzy that is manifested in Memorial Hall's striated elevations.

The icing on this massive layer cake is the exceptional decoration of its surface. The carvings of the Ruskinian Gothic Memorial Hall pale desperately in comparision with the fine embellishment on the capitals of Austin Hall. Intertwined in foliage are tiny faces, such as that of a wizened old woman wearing a bonnet, or a yawning man in his nightcap. Directly beneath these comic images are a legion of carved animals, each no more than two inches across, which are almost completely obscured by both the stone foliage and, unfortunately, by acid rain deterioration. Owls, dragonflies and crustaceans are but a few of them. Above the capitals an elegant transition to the entry arches occurs in delicately carved, almost Celtic patterns of interlaced textural elements incorporated with medieval dragon figures and stylized foliage. The surface created by Richardson and his craftsmen could be no more lively or visually satisfying.

John T. O'Connor

Detail, Austin Hall, c. 1885 from *Monographs of American Architecture I*

Hampden Hall, the rusticated brick and granite building at Eight Plympton Street, represents the era of the "Gold Coast," or private, dormitory. Ushered in by Harvard's President Charles Eliot, who vowed not to authorize construction of any undergraduate housing during his tenure, the resulting private residence halls were much more lavish in many respects than University-built housing. Designed by the firm Coolidge and Carlson in 1901–02, Hampden Hall was closest to Harvard Yard, facing both Dexter Gate and Gore Hall. The plan of the building and a photograph of the façade were illustrated in *The American Architect*, July 1903. According to that publication, what stands today is only a portion of what was to be constructed. The other half of the building presumably was to extend down Massachusetts Avenue to the corner of Bow Street. Shown here is a carved granite keystone of elaborate workmanship that rests above the hall's massive entrance. It contains the grotesque face of a grinning, fantastic creature, and a small fish below.

John T. O'Connor

Keystone, granite, Hampden Hall, Coolidge and Carlson, architects, 1901

The stone griffins near the entrance of the Frances Loeb Library in Gund Hall once stood on the roof of the original Fogg Museum of Art. Richard Morris Hunt designed them in 1893 as ornaments of that building, which became an annex of the Graduate School of Design when the present Fogg Museum opened in 1928. It was renamed Hunt Hall to honor its architect in 1935, and was torn down in 1973 to make way for Canaday Hall, when various fragments found their way to Gund Hall, which houses the Graduate School of Design. In 1852, while Hunt studied at the Ecole des Beaux Arts in Paris, Charles Garnier prepared his envoi for that school, a reconstruction of the Temple of Jupiter at Aegina, fifth century B.C., which includes similar, but brightly colored griffins on acroteria at opposite ends of the pediment.

The griffins belong to the family of creatures, some invented, some historic, which guard many Harvard buildings: the rhinoceri at the entrance of the Biological Laboratories, the boar above the Porcellian Gate, and the orators over the windows of Sanders Theatre. Mythological combinations of a lion's body with an eagle's head, griffins are of ancient, near-eastern origin. Their links to the distant past are rich but their meaning for us today is obscure. The Hunt Hall griffins did not hear Sabine's famous experiments on acoustics in the lecture hall beneath their post, and they cannot tell us what theories of art and architecture Norton taught there. Ghosts of many lost buildings remain only in drawings and photographs inside the library; if pieces of these buildings are recycled to new homes, they haunt the occupants with thoughts that much more has been lost than was saved.

Christopher Hail

Griffin, limestone, from Original William Hayes Fogg Museum (Hunt Hall), R.M. Hunt, architect, 1893

Detail, Busch-Reisinger Museum, 1916, German Bestelmeyer

Detail, Busch-Reisinger Museum, 1916, German Bestelmeyer

The unstudied opulence, the whimsical flourishes, and the playful eccentricities of Warren and Wetmore's turn-of-the-century design for Westmorely Court on Bow Street were perfectly suited to the wealthy young men seeking luxurious Gold Coast living at the beginning of the century. Cylindrical vestibules, sit-in fireplaces, and linen-fold-paneled doors are a few of the eclectic details within the walls of these sumptuous quarters for a fortunate handful of Harvard students during Charles William Eliot's presidency.

Behind a narrow wooden door off an anonymous hallway is what may best epitomize the decadence of the time: the natatorium. Descending marble stairs, one removes one's slippers to feel the brisk cold of terra cotta tiles, enters and glides through pristinely clear water toward the north end of the pool. Upon surfacing, one is greeted by a rush of water falling from above, spewing forth from the mouth of an image of a bearded old man. The limestone countenance appears to be that of Poseidon, who at one time watched soberly over the antics of privileged gentlemen splashing about in an age when pleasure was paramount, and long before their secret pond became the Adams House swimming pool in 1930.

Plans in the 1960s to convert the facility into a theater were abandoned, and although the fountain has fallen into disrepair, the sea god continues to cast his expressionless gaze over the occasional visitor.

Stanford Makishi

Fountain, limestone, Westmorley Court pool, Warren & Wetmore, architects, 1898

Built by the City of Cambridge, on land essential to the visual link between Harvard Yard and North Yard, this fire station extends the continuity of the Neo-Georgian brick and cut-stone architecture, so much in vogue for Harvard construction of the era. Designed by R. Clipston Sturgis, Class of 1881, the building contains one element that reflects more closely conditions of the 1930s. Unusual keystones that crown the three arched truck entrances have the decided flavor of the depression-period Work Progress Administration.

Within the volutes of these limestone wedges are the representations of firemen, one with hose, one with axe and the central figure grasping a ladder. Each wears the wide-brimmed helmets and heavy coats that hint distinctly at the era of the building. One is reminded here of other W.P.A. projects, in particular the fire station at Coral Gables, Florida, in which carved coral blocks depict both firemen and the various entities they protect; dogs, cats, boys, girls. The keystones on the Cambridge fire station combine exacting revival detail with whimsy, becoming in the process very accessible and altogether human.

John T. O'Connor

Keystone, Cambridge Fire Station, 1933, R. Clipston Sturgis, architect

PRINT

The field of Graphic Design in the 20th century deals with the decisive manipulation of typographic and illustrative elements for the printed page. Prior to the 20th century there were typographers, engravers and printers, but no recognized profession. In spite of this, or perhaps because of it, printed works at Harvard, throughout its history, display great diversity and virtuosity. One need only peek under the cover of various books in the stacks of Widener Library to discover the most exquisitely engraved book-plates—from 18th century baroque cartouches to the severe Swiss style of this century. Design commissioned by the departments within the University is often excellent, and one hopes Harvard can continue its supportive role as the catalyst of good design.

Bookplate, c. 1780 5½″ × 3¼″ engraving, Nathaniel Hurd

In 1857 Harvard College received from the bequest of Francis Calley Gray, Class of 1809, the first great collection of old-master prints to be formed in America. The Corporation of the College hired Louis Thies as the collection's curator, a German connoisseur who earlier had been Gray's agent. Thies, like Gray, thought little of American engraving. He therefore commissioned a College seal from the engraver to the court of Dresden, the capital of Saxony, at a cost of $15.85 for the purpose of decorating the Gray Collection catalogue. The Print of Cabinet in Dresden was among the most famous in Europe and decades earlier had inspired Thies to devote his life to prints. Furthermore, King John of Saxony was an intellectual monarch with literary tastes who had translated Dante and corresponded with such Harvard professors as George Ticknor, Gray's closest friend.

The design of the seal conformed to that advocated by Edward Everett, another of Gray's Boston Brahmin friends, who while president of Harvard had rejected a design promoted by his predecessor Josiah Quincy, yet another friend of Gray. On the occasion of Harvard's bicentennial in 1836, when President Quincy was writing the history of the College, he had rediscovered in the College records the original seal design from 1643, which included the motto "VERITAS" inscribed on three books. In the intervening centuries, "VERITAS" had been forgotten, the books were left blank, and "Christos et Ecclesiae" appeared as an inscription. In the 1870s, Quincy's "VERITAS" and Everett's blank books with "Christos et Ecclesiae" became the symbols around which rallied, respectively, the liberal and conservative factions among alumni newly interested in the College arms. Satirical sonnets published in 1878 by Oliver Wendell Holmes, Sr., tipped the balance for "VERITAS," and by 1885 the blank books were inscribed once more and the definitive Harvard arms established. This elegant rendering of the earlier seal is our most visible reminder of the controversy of a century ago.

Marjorie Cohn

George Jahn   *Harvard College Seal*, 1868, 41 mm diam., decoration of the cover and title page of *Catalogue of the Collection of Engravings Bequeathed to Harvard College by Francis Calley Gray*, Louis Thies (Cambridge: Welch, Bigelow, and Company, printers to the University, 1869).

When the university decided to abandon the individually engrossed Latin diploma, its replacement in 1961 drew many objections; so many, that the committee responsible for it turned to a seasoned, renowned designer, Rudolph Ruzicka, for a new design. Its continued use through the last quarter century attests to its effectiveness.

Ruzicka took time to study the variables posed by different schools, lengths of names and degrees. The spare, open design is straightforwardly a piece of printed matter, not posing as a calligraphic dupe, clearly legible in large sizes of two distinguished typefaces: *Centaur* and *Bembo. Centaur* (designed by Bruce Rogers) is subtly decorative in the unusual shaping of the body of the capital letters and in the exaggerated serif bracketings. The balanced diploma design is enriched at opposite corners by the Harvard seal, die-stamped over a preprinted circle of light buff-colored ink, and at the upper left by Ruzicka's dense, oak leaf cluster (it is more open, branch-like, and not so stylized in the original sketch) with open books bearing "Veritas" in letters of his own design. The color is burnt sienna, not Harvard crimson, which he felt would have overpowered the typography.

Ruzicka had a long and distinguished career as a graphic artist. He learned metal engraving as a teenager in Chicago, and mastered the demanding craft of wood engraving as a young man. He loved ornament based on natural forms and invented unorthodox pastel color combinations to enhance his superb engravings. Nevertheless, he let neither ornament nor color run away with the design; he kept all in balance, an enriched whole.

Carl Zahn

HARVARD UNIVERSITY

AT CAMBRIDGE IN THE COMMONWEALTH OF MASSACHUSETTS

VE RI TAS

THE President and Fellows of Harvard College, with the consent of the Honorable and Reverend the Board of Overseers and acting on the recommendation of the Faculty of Arts and Sciences, have conferred on

ARTURO FRANCISCO COLORADO-MANITOBA

the degree of Bachelor of Science.

In witness whereof, *by authority duly committed to us, we have hereunder placed our names and the seal of the University on this fourteenth day of June in the Year of Our Lord nineteen hundred and sixty-two and of Harvard College the three hundred and twenty-sixth.*

Nathan Marsh Pusey
PRESIDENT

DEAN OF THE COLLEGE

MASTER

The Diploma of Harvard Univeristy, letterpress with embossed seal, 1962, Rudolph Ruzicka

Bookplate, 1906, 4½″ × 3¼″ copper engraving, Frederick Garrison Hall

Bookplate, c. 1900 4″ × 3¼″ copper engraving, Ernest Clegg for American Bank Note Co.

The use of heraldic arms to adorn Harvard buildings is by no means new. As early as 1699, graduate of the Class of 1650 Governor Stoughton's arms, now vanished, appeared on the facade of Old Stoughton Hall, which was completed from his gift in that year and finally torn down in 1781.

The earliest arms surviving on a Harvard building are those located over the original entrance at the west end of Holden Chapel, completed in 1744. In wood, they are surrounded by an elaborate "mantling" and depict the arms of Holden in a square resting on one corner, i.e., in a "hatchment" signifying a widow. At the center of the Holden arms is imposed a "shield of pretense," signifying a rich wife, with the arms of Jane Holden née Whitehall, who was the widow of an English merchant, Samuel Holden. Her two daughters gave 400 pounds for the construction of the Chapel. The arms were reproduced over the present entrance at the west end, probably at the instigation of President Lowell, Class of 1877, sometime between 1913 and the early 1920s.

Heraldic arms began to appear in greater numbers on or in Harvard's buildings in various forms and materials during the 19th century. The decorative arms of the Signet Society were designed by Pierre la Rose, Class of 1895, and placed over the front door when the Society acquired its present house in 1901. Moreover, for Harvard's Tercentenary in 1936, Pierre la Rose designed arms for the various Graduate Schools to be displayed on banners that decorated the Tercentenary Theater, and that have often been used since to decorate buildings of the Schools. These arms generally represent a family concerned in the founding of the School in question, although in one or two cases the arms were invented by la Rose. At the top of the arms of the Graduate Schools, la Rose placed a "chief of Harvard," which is a red band bearing in gold the three open books inscribed with "VE-RI-TAS."

When the residential Houses for students were started by President Lowell from the gift of Mr. Edward Harkness, each took for its arms those of the family of the person for whom it was named, whether these arms were genuinely of the family, only putatively so, or, in two

Arms of
Lowell House
in Harvard College

cases, invented for the occasion. The arms of Lowell House, one of the first two Houses opened in 1930, are perhaps displayed in the most lofty position, namely on pediments on the north and south faces of the tower that rises above the main entrance to the House. They are the arms of an English family named Lowle, and were apparently first used in this country, by the descendant of an immigrant who spelled his name Lowell: Reverend John Lowell, Class of 1721, pastor in Newbury, Massachusetts, during the mid-18th century.

Although the official practice of the University is to display only a shield without crest or motto, Lowell House uses all three elements. The field of the shield is black, although it is at present erroneously painted blue on the tower. On the shield, all in white, a right hand cut off at the wrist grasps three short and blunted arrows or darts, with feathers up and points down, or which the center one is vertical and the other two slant across it from either side. The crest is a gold stag's head facing front and cut off at the neck. Between the horns is a blue lance head. The head rests on a heraldic pad, whose visible edge resembles a cord of twisted gold and black strands, the colors of the arms. The motto beneath the shield, in gold on a black ribbon, reads: *Occasionem Cognosce*, i.e., "Know the Opportunity" (or the Right Time), which supposedly inspired President Lowell to remark: "Take the Harkness gift when offered." The President referred to the fact that, before Mr. Harkness made his gift to Harvard for the Houses, he had offered it to Yale, which never even responded. This motto may well have been adopted first by the Reverend John Lowell as Latin version of a Greek motto attributed to the early sage Pittacus (ca. 600 B.C.), in English letters: *Kaicon Gnosthe*, or "Know the Right Time."

Mason Hammond

During Elliot Perkin's tenure as Master of Lowell House, three enormous, cut-crystal chandeliers were hung from the great high ceiling of the House's dining hall. The brilliance of the prisms attests to their craftsmanship, and because they make such excellent use of the abundant daylight, they are well suited to the large room with its tall, semicircular-topped windows that run the length of the north and south walls. Unlike most of the older Houses, whose dining halls are paneled, Lowell's dining hall has pristine white walls that contribute to a feeling of airy openness, enhanced by a black- and white-checked floor.

The chandeliers may have been originally intended as replacements for the drab wooden chandeliers in Eliot House's dining hall. Legend has it that the glass company delivery men were mistakenly directed to Elliot Perkins rather than to Eliot House. When informed of the nature of the truckers' cargo, Master Perkins no doubt saw a rare opportunity and directed the men to Lowell's dining hall. Installation began immediately, and by day's end the glistening fixtures were in place in their pavilion-like setting, ever after to lend an element of sophistication and pomp to Lowell's famous "High Table" luncheons and dinners. By the time the powers-that-were of Eliot House had found out about the misrouting of their own chandeliers, the mistake and subsequent intrigue were already well on the way to becoming part of Harvard tradition. For Lowell House, the lavish chandeliers will always be a source both of illumination and of pride in the House, and an inspiration to take to heart what might well have been Master Perkins's motto: *"Carpe diem"* (Seize the day).

Lorcan O'Neill

Chandelier (one of three), lead crystal, c. 1931, manufacturer unknown

In the spring of 1891 Edward Emerson Simmons, Class of 1874, and a graduate of the Ecole des Beaux Arts, left his painting studio in Paris to undertake the task of designing and supervising, for the Tiffany Glass and Decorating Company, the execution of this window in the great hall of Memorial Hall. His class had the unique distinction of being the only class to donate a window designed and completed by a fellow classmate.

The subject is the reconciliation of Themistocles and Aristeides, two Athenians who were rivals but rallied together in the cause to save Greece from the invasion of Xerxes. Herodotus (8:79.81) tells us that the night before the battle of Salamis in 480 B.C. the ostracized Aristeides, impelled to the defense of his country in a time of adversity, returned through enemy lines from exile on the island of Aegina to make amends with Themistocles. Since Memorial Hall commemorates all Harvard men who served in the Union forces of the Civil War, it is appropriate to evoke this classical image, especially in light of the reconciliation of the North and South nine years prior to the commencement of the Class of 1874.

The text from Herodotus that describes the actual reconciliation is started on the window, but by some odd quirk is not completed—as the empty cartouche on the right panel suggests.

ὡς δὲ ἐξῆλθέ οἱ θεμιστοκλέης, ἔλεγε Ἀριστείδης τάδε.
" Ἡμέας στασιάζειν χρεόν ἐστι ἔν τε ἄλλῳ [καιρῷ καὶ δὴ
ἐν τῷδε περὶ τοῦ ὁκότερος ἡμῶν πλέω ἀγαθὰ τὴν πατρίδα
ἐργάσεται]."

The Greek in brackets is undoubtedly what was to be inscribed to complete the inscription. Translated, the inscription in its final form would have read as follows:

Stained glass, Memorial Hall, Tiffany Glass and
Decorating Co., 1874

"and when Themistocles came out to him Aristeides said the following; It is necessary that the rivalry between us be now as it has been before, to see which of us two shall do his country more good"

The committee for the Class of 1894 (p. 84) states " . . . when it is remembered that our class numbers among its members, men who proved their devotion to the respective causes of the North and South by service in the field, the appropriateness of the subject still becomes more striking." Yet this is the only reference to the Confederate soldiers throughout Memorial Hall. As late as 1978, efforts to commemorate the Confederate Harvardians were quashed. This unfortunate situation is perpetuated by the preamble of the document which transferred Memorial Hall from the Alumni Association to the President and Fellows of Harvard College and specifically states that its purpose is for those who died in defense of the Union. The Class of 1874, as Harvard historian Professor Mason Hammond points out, was way ahead of its time since to date there is no official memorial within the Hall recognizing the Crimson Confederates.

James L. Healy, Jr.

Detail of stained glass, Class of 1874 window, Memorial Hall, Tiffany Glass and Decorating Co.

Decorative scenes of Harvard were used during the early 19th century by Staffordshire potteries in England (excluding Wedgwood) on plates and other pieces of ceramic, usually in series depicting views of American places. In the 1830s, President Josiah Quincy, Class of 1790, purchased a large number of plates, bowls and other pieces of this ware in blue for the College Dining Halls, then located in University Hall.

During the last years of the 19th century and early part of the 20th, ceramic objects portraying the Harvard arms or Harvard scenes began to be produced for sale to students (as they still are), chiefly by U.S. firms but occasionally by Wedgwood.

In 1926, President Lowell, Class of 1877, decided to have a set of twelve dinner plates depicting Harvard scenes made to be sold by the Alumni Association. He chose Professor Kenneth J. Conant, Class of 1915, to execute the drawings, and Wedgwood to manufacture the plates. When Conant brought his drawings to Lowell to be approved, he found the President in a hole dug for the new heat tunnel located just off the southeast corner of University Hall; excavation of the tunnel had unearthed the dump of the 19th-century kitchens, which contained many fragments of Quincy's Staffordshire ware. Lowell was able to obtain elsewhere an intact plate from this line, which was sent to Wedgwood to provide the color and border pattern for the newly commissioned plates. The set of twelve dinner plates went on sale in 1927 and was so successful that many other U.S. educational institutions adopted the idea, and at Harvard various sets of individual pieces continued to be made through 1951, chiefly with designs by Conant and in both red and blue.

When the residential Houses opened in the early 1930s, special china for some was made by U.S. firms. Lowell House, for example, selected for its china a view of its large courtyard

Luncheon plate, 8″ diameter, crimson on white Wedgewood, c. 1934

and tower, and Kirkland House chose its arms, designed by Pierre la Rose, Class of 1895.

Probably the most impressive piece produced by Wedgwood for the Alumni Association was a punch bowl executed in red and blue in honor of the Tercentenary of 1936. Wedgwood used as a model a 19th-century Liverpool bowl in sepia, loaned by a member of the committee in charge of the project. Wedgwood also produced a limited number of the Harvard bowl in sepia for the committee members. Around the inside top of the punch bowl is a floral border and on the interior bottom is shown the 1736 Burgis view of the college buildings across from the Old Burying Ground. On the outside, one side portrays the Quincy 1836 view of the College and the other shows a view by Professor Conant of the Houses along the Charles River. In both spaces between these views are three versions of the Harvard arms, as explained on a list along the bowl's outside bottom.

Mason Hammond

Salad plate, 7″ diameter, crimson and grey on white ironstone, c. 1931

Located in the Whitman Room of Radcliffe's Arthur and Elizabeth Schlesinger Library on the History of Women in America, this striking stained glass window was designed and executed by Sarah Wyman Whitman (1842–1904), for whom Whitman Hall is named. The window depicts the virtues of Courage, Love and Patience. Reminiscent of the English Pre-Raphaelite School, it reflects in its coloration and tone Mrs. Whitman's study with the painter William Morris Hunt.

Made specifically for the St. Louis World's Fair, the window was given to Radcliffe to honor Whitman's deep friendship with Elizabeth Cary Agassiz, and her abiding interest in the Society for the Collegiate Instruction of Women, as Radcliffe was originally called. The window was first installed in Agassiz House and was subsequently moved in 1907 to the Radcliffe Library, newly built at that time. There it resides today, illuminating a corner of Radcliffe heritage and history while also highlighting the creativity, talent and achievement of 19th-century American women, whose lives are documented in Schlesinger Library.

Matina Horner

Stained glass, Sarah Wyman Whitman, c. 1904

Open a certain nondescript door marked "Private" in the Fogg Museum, and you will enter into the dignified tranquillity of the Naumburg Rooms. Sometimes a solitary figure reading a newspaper is lounging, or a luncheon or tea is taking place—activities perfectly in accord with Mrs. Naumburg's intention that the rooms serve as living rooms within the museum. Comprised of a small entrance hall, dining room, living room with balcony, and stairway, the rooms were bequeathed to Harvard in 1930; the walls with English Jacobean paneling, ceilings, floors, and windows and stained glass were brought from the Naumburgs' New York home and installed. Paintings, sculptures and tapestries were part of the bequest, as well as $100,000 for installation and $25,000 for maintenance. The new wing housing this gift opened to the public on November 10, 1932, and closed one month later, thenceforth to be used only by Harvard students, faculty and staff.

The rooms are venerable and ornate, but reflect years of use. Set within a simple pattern of clear glass rectangles, the stained glass panels of the windows located above the stair landing are in the best condition. A scholar named Ann Fitzgerald, now deceased, worked on cataloguing the glass for the Fogg, ca. 1935. The Swiss glass appears to date from the late 16th and early 17th centuries. Window No. 2, reproduced here, was described by Fitzgerald in her unpublished catalogue. Biblical in subject, it portrays on pediments St. John the Baptist and his lamb at upper left, and St. James the Great with book and staff at upper right. Betwen them, Jacob is shown struggling with the Angel in the foreground of a rural landscape; in the background a caravan with horses and camels fords a river. Below this is written "Genesis A.M. XXXII cap," beneath which appears a jester's puppet at left and a device at right. At left and right of the central portion of the panel are Jacob and Esau. Between them are two ornate shields, one blue and one gold, the latter at right emblazoned with the unidentified device above. In lozenges, flanked by busts and angels at the panel's bottom, appear the inscriptions: "Hans Jacob Payer und" (left), and "Dorothea Payerin Ein Ceborne Payerin in Hoff Sein Ehg ma 1606 hel" (right). Although the scenes are unambitious and simply rendered, the beautiful glass glows in richly varied tones.

Julie Collins

Detail of stained glass in the Aaron and Nettie C. Naumburg Rooms, early 17th-century

Sever Hall presides—even looms—over the Yard, communicating through its imposing mass and varied, but balanced silhouette. One can imagine that if H. H. Richardson were asked that ponderous, 19th-century question: "What is the Just Subordination, in Architectural Design, of Detail to Mass?", he might have answered: "Total Subordination." But of course, there is much more to Sever Hall than its mass. It also has detail, or ornament, that can instruct, entertain, amuse, excite or act upon us in countless ways. While this is true, it can be said of many of the buildings designed by Richardson's contemporaries. What distinguishes Richardson's architecture, at least once he left what he called his "pyrotechnic" phrase, is the supple way that his ornament creates graceful transitions between the major building elements—between window and wall, door and wall, roof and cornice, front and side, and so on. The elements are vitalized in the process, and through this charged interplay, Sever Hall becomes much more than a building. It is then also a construct of such power and intricacy that it can be used by analogy to illuminate any aspect of mental and emotional discourse. As such, it is hard to imagine a more fitting building at the center of a university campus.

David Handlin

Sever Hall, sketch from the office of H.H. Richardson, c. 1878, from the collection at Houghton library, Harvard University

I am immensely grateful to Sever Hall: It has taught me that ornament does not imply the mechanical repetition of an element underlining the order within the building structure, or entail the superficial application of recognizable elements on the bulk of the building mass. Moreover, Sever Hall has shown me that ornament is not the authoritarian expression of the designer. Despite the fact that Sever Hall's ornament appears to be subjugated to architectural forms, in reality it is liberated for the work of the artist.

I imagine the sculptor walking on the scaffolding, moving from one subject to another, never mechanically repeating his gestures, and eager to finish a bunch of grapes in order to begin work on a stalk of wheat. Our eyes are captured by a variety that has nothing to do with the picturesque; by a variety that retains in its singularity the autonomy of each detail carved in the brick. Furthermore, Sever Hall rejects the idea of ornament as merely epidermal enrichment. On this building, Richardson wanted to demonstrate that ornament is not something aggregated or applied, but instead is capable of sharing in the substance—the very matter—of the building itself.

I love to see the hall's carved brick. It speaks to me about the manner in which the building accepts its ornament. Sever Hall incorporates this final moment in the building process without renouncing any aspect of its wholeness, or therefore the need of carving. As a result, we are touched by the white joints of mortar running through the eyes of the owl as well as on the ivy leaves. A phantom appears, almost lost in the mass of the gently carved bricks: the shield of Harvard, to which Richardson seems to have dedicated this work.

José Rafael Moneo

Detail, carved brick, Sever Hall, 1880, H.H. Richardson, architect

"When I consider Thy heavens, the work of Thy fingers, the moon
and the stars, which Thou hast ordained; What is Man, that Thou
art mindful of him?"

Psalms 8:4

For Josiah Royce, William James, George Santayana and their colleagues, this quotation related their new building explicitly to Harvard's Ralph Waldo Emerson, after whom it was named. For the prestigious Philosophy Department of Harvard University in 1901, this signage perfectly expressed their aspirations for the human mind. It symbolized the confidence of William James, who articulated the doctrine of Pragmatism to provide an American beacon on the horizon of human thought in the decadent age of the *Art Nouveau*.

The Greek ideal of the perfectability of man exemplified Harvard thinking around 1900, and was an ideal to which many contributed. Harvard's classical stadium of 1902 in part was made possible through an affiliation of physical education with the divisions of Classics and Philosophy. In 1899 at the first Council of the National Convention of the American Association for the Advancement of Physical Education, held at Harvard, William James was among those who spoke in favor of the sound mind in the sound body.

With its terra cotta ornament, Emerson Hall demonstrates a perfect confluence of structure and design. As John Ruskin said:

"[Terra cotta] excels every other [material] in permanence, and,
perhaps, requires even greater skill in its management than marble . . . A piece of terra cotta . . . which has been wrought by human hand, is worth all the stone in Carrara cut by machinery."

The Sever Quadrangle had been projected by H. H. Richardson as early as 1879, and was completed during 1902–1904 with the erection of Emerson and Robinson Halls. Guy Low-

Emerson Hall, north facade, 1900, Guy Lowell, architect

ell's contained, yet powerful design for Emerson deferred to both the rectilinear disposition of Sever and Harvard Yard to the west. In its use of brick Emerson extends the continuum from the 18th century that inspired the east door of Sever Hall, but its vigor embodies late 19th-century classical ideals. The great brick columns rising to the Ionic capitals and ebullient inscribed entablature of terra cotta provide the ultimate synthesis of the design. For if man is clay, then the man-fired ornament that is embedded in the structure of Emerson Hall embodies the philosophical ideals of its inhabitants. The great age of terra cotta in modern architecture is best expressed at Harvard in Emerson Hall, a building in the Yard dedicated to humanism.

Margaret Henderson Floyd

Emerson Hall, Guy Lowell, architect, 1900

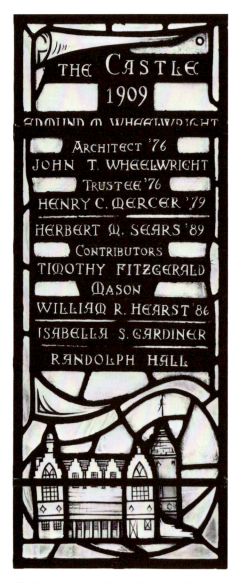

Detail of stained glass, Harvard Lampoon, 1909,
Wheelwright and Haven, architects

Detail of terra-cotta trim, Weld Boathouse, 1906, Robert Peabody, architect

About the Contributors

John Timothy O'Connor B.F.A.
Currently involved in graduate study at
Harvard University Graduate School of Design

Louise Todd Ambler A.B.
Curator of the Harvard University Portrait
Collection, Fogg Art Museum

Henry N. Cobb A.B., M.ARCH
Adjunct Professor of Architecture and Urban
Design
Founding Partner, I.M. Pei & Partners, N.Y.

Marjorie B. Cohn B.A., A.M.
Conservator of Works of Art on Paper in the
Harvard University Art Museums

Julia Mary Collins B.A.
Currently involved in graduate study at
Columbia University

Victoria Crowninshield Drake A.B.
Currently involved in research at the
Coolidge Center for Environmental Leadership

William Drake A.B. M.AR.
Partner, Skidmore, Owings & Merrill, Chicago

Margaret Floyd
Professor, Department of Fine Arts
Tufts University

Christopher Hail B.A.
Assistant Librarian in the
Graduate School of Design

Mason Hammond A.B., B.A., B.LITT.,
LITT.D.
Pope Professor of the Latin Language and Litera-
ture, Emeritus, Honorary Associate and Master of
Kirkland House, Emeritus

David Handlin A.B. DIPL. M.ARCH M.A.
Principle, David P. Handlin and Associates

James L. Healy, Jr. A.L.B.
Currently involved in graduate study at
Bryn Mawr College

Matina Souretis Horner B.A., M.SC., PH.D.
President of Radcliffe College
Associate Professor of Psychology and Social
Relations

Stanford N. Makishi A.B. ('87)
Undergraduate, Harvard College

José Rafael Moneo DIPL. ARCH., DR.
Chairman, Department of Architecture
Professor of Architecture

Peter Nisbet B.A., M.A., M.PHIL.
Assistant Curator of the Busch-Reisinger
Museum in the Harvard University Art Museums

A. Lorcan O'Neill A.B.
Associate Director, Barbara Krakow Gallery,
Boston, MA

Carl Zahn A.B.
Director of Publications
Museum of Fine Arts, Boston

Illustrations

All photography is by Rod Dresser unless listed below:

Cover: Kenneth Hilgendorf

Page 6:   Harvard University Art Museums

Page 9:   Harvard University Art Museums

Page 13:   Harvard University Art Museums

Page 17:   Harvard University Art Museums

Page 20:   New York Historical Society, N.Y.C.

Page 23:   Monographs of American Architecture, J. Osgood and Co. 1887 Harvard University Archives

Page 25:   Monographs of American Architecture, J. Osgood and Co. 1887 Harvard University Archives

Page 31:   New York Historical Society, N.Y.C.

Page 38:   Houghton Library, Harvard University

Page 41:   Harvard University Art Museums

Page 43:   Houghton Library, Harvard University

Page 44:   Courtesy Harvard University Graduate School of Design

Page 45:   Courtesy Harvard Business School

Page 55:   Class Report of 1894/Harvard University Archives

Page 71:   Harvard University Archives

Acknowledgments

I would like to thank the following people for all their help in producing this book, especially Louise Ambler for her unerring advice and constant support; Robin McElheny for sharing her considerable research, not to mention her time; Julie Collins for her manuscript editing, and finally Margi Reeve, without her drive and support this book would not have been published.

Louise Todd Ambler, Curator of the Harvard University Portrait Collection

Marjorie Cohn, Director of Conservation, Harvard University Art Museums

Julia Mary Collins, Publications Editor, Graduate School of Design

Rodney Dennis, Curator of Manuscripts, Harvard College Library

Rod Dresser, photographer

Eleanor Garvey, Curator of Printing and Graphic Arts, Harvard College Library

Mason Hammond, Pope Professor of Latin Language and Literature, Emeritus

James L Healy, Jr. A.L.B. '86

Robert A. Humphreville, A.B. '80

Stanford Makishi, A.B. '87

Robin McElheny, Curatorial Associate for Visual Collections, University Archives

Susan McNally, Publications Coordinator, Graduate School of Design

Cynthia Naylor, Houghton Library, Harvard University

Catherine O'Connor, Department of Linguistics, University of California, Berkeley

Margaret Reeve, Curator of Exhibitions, Graduate School of Design

Richard Stafford, Photographer, Harvard University Art Museums

Design: John T. O'Connor   Typography: Rainsford Type   Printing: Thomas Todd Company